CHAR
REVIEWED

A Philosophy of Education

Jenny King

Child Light Publication

First published in Great Britain, 1981

This edition published 2000 by Child Light Ltd.
P.O. Box 59, Petersfield. Hants. GU32 3YL

ISBN
0-9538072-1-5

Printed and bound in Great Britain by
Antony Rowe Ltd, Chippenham, Wiltshire

Contents

Preface to the Second Edition

I have a copy of "*School Education*" by Charlotte Mason in front of me, originally published in 1907. In the preface she says, "The educational outlook is rather misty and depressing....That science should be a staple of education...that education must be made more technical and utilitarian....these, and such as these, are the cries of expedience with which we take the field." She goes on to say though, that we have no "unifying principle, no definite aim, no philosophy of education."

In her writings based on practical experience in the classroom she describes what might be called a philosophy of education.

"We are dealing with *persons* and must provide an atmosphere, a discipline, and a life, by developing education as a science of relationships."

We can therefore be technical and scientific and even utilitarian, but always bearing in mind the spiritual nature of Homo Sapiens.

Jenny King C.M.T.
Reading, England 2000

Foreword

It is a privilege to be asked to write a foreword to this excellent little book concerning the educationalist Charlotte Mason.

It was perhaps unfortunate that Charlotte Mason was so strongly averse to the use of her own name. This gave rise to the ugly letters PNEU. Today it is ironic that only her *name* remains! For the State College to which it is attached cannot follow her philosophy of education though the Principal and his staff greatly revere her memory.

And now there comes to the fore Jenny King's little book which puts before us with admirable clarity and real understanding the essential principles and practices of this great woman. I like the arrangement Miss King has chosen to follow. It is fresh, clear, and to the point.

To Charlotte Mason the Christian Faith was the essential centre and pivot of her work. Moreover she was insistent that morality and individual behaviour follow personal belief. She writes admirably in *Parents and Children* on this important subject, for the argument 'he can choose and decide for himself when old enough' was nearly as lively in her day as it is common today. And consequently as Miss King says —

little children to whom it is so natural to turn to their Heavenly Father are weighted with the bias of ignorance and deprived of the joy of living in the presence of God.

The nourishing of the mind through the reading and narration of well-written books is not easily understood without training. Indeed, I can say that this particular aspect of the training in the Practising School at Ambleside was usually the last to be grasped. As a Lecturer in Education in several State Colleges, I have never found any educationalist to touch Charlotte Mason on her understanding of the work of the mind. Her students learnt to express themselves in good English and to speak well. I doubt if the English language has ever been at a lower ebb than it is today!

I believe that Jenny King's book has come to us just when most needed, not only to tell those unfamiliar with Charlotte Mason about her work, but also to remind her old students — many of whom are now elderly — that she still stands alone in her philosophy of education centred in the Christian Faith and if ever she could be followed what a revolution in education would take place in the country!

Joyce van Straubenzee (CMT Recognized)
(Diploma in Education[Lond.])
Principal of the Charlotte Mason College 1937-1955

Part One Section One

Introduction

'We have no unifying principle, no definite aim; in fact no philosophy of education.' This quotation comes from a series of books on education in the home and the school written by Charlotte Mason and published between 1886 and 1922.

In some ways our present age is very like the late nineteenth centry. State education was still quite new and a lively debate about curricula and methods was occupying the minds of those engaged in the education of the nation's children. New political forces were demanding the attention of government and a general awakening of the working class to their economic power was concerning the heads of industry.

As we reach the last twenty years of the present century the picture does not change much. The great educational debate is still with us. Political forces of which we have little understanding are subverting the establishment. The Trade Union movement has engulfed the workers of every trade and industry so that what started as a murmur one hundred years ago has become a roaring of demands which threaten to overthrow society.

A hundred years ago the gentle voice of Charlotte Mason was heard and listened to by many people interested in a liberal education for all. It is the purpose of this book to record that voice anew because we still have no unifying principle, no definite aim, no philosophy of education.

We are surrounded by voices crying first for one reform and then for another, a little here and a little there. Energies and finances are dissipated in a welter of theory, while what we seek, an education which draws out the best of every child and builds a nation of responsible citizens, eludes us at every turn of the road.

The solution to our problems does not lie in more nursery schools, bigger comprehensives, a return to 'Eleven Plus' and the re-establishment of grammar schools. It lies in the child himself.

This does not mean the 'progressive' theory of child-centredness advocated by those who believe that the child knows best what he should learn and when. It is something much more significant — the realization that a child is born a person.

Neither will our problems be banished by the thinking which says that education must be utilitarian, that skills required in adult life should be taught in school. There are other and better ways of training the future workforce particularly at a time when the 'three day week' is likely to become a permanent situation. 'A nation that allows materialism to dictate the education of her children is doomed to disintegration.'

Charlotte Mason spoke of an 'educational revolution' — not a revolution which destroys but one which turns itself round and faces essentials, gets its priorities right and builds on a philosophy based on principles which are fundamental to the good of the child and the welfare of the nation.

The purpose of this account of the work of Charlotte Mason is to put into the hands of parents and teachers a philosophy of education which if followed will help them to find a solution to the problems that face all educators in every generation — how to make the most of the potential in every child.

Charlotte Mason who was born in 1842 and died in 1923 knew what it was to be without means long before the advent of the Welfare State. Left an orphan at sixteen she was entirely dependent on friends for shelter and financial support. Teaching was the only opening for a young woman in those times and Charlotte Mason determined to devote her life to education and particularly to the children of the poor. In 1860 she became a student at the only training college at that time in the country under the auspices of the Home and Colonial Society. In 1874 Charlotte was appointed Vice-Principal of the Bishop Otter Training College for Teachers in Chichester. Later she lived and worked in Bradford and it was here that the Parents' National Educational Union was formed in 1887.

All through her life Charlotte Mason concerned herself with the nation's children — not only the children of the upper and middle classes. She lectured widely and wrote books for use in schools as well as those devoted to her philosophy of education. In 1892 the first students assembled at 'Springfield' in Ambleside to be trained at Charlotte Mason's own college. At the age of fifty she was just starting on a new venture, viz., the training college for teachers — having already founded the Parents' Union, and the Parents' Union School!

It is difficult to realize that these tremendous undertakings had all sprung from the efforts of a penniless orphan girl of sixteen, especially one who was dogged by ill health all her life and had to take long periods of rest from time to time. A full account of her life is written elsewhere and through the incidents which are recorded flows the divine inspiration which she recognized so fully. Her creed is expressed in the fresco depicting the descent of the Holy Spirit in the Spanish Chapel of Santa Maria in Florence. Here all the liberal arts and sciences are represented as the result of the outpouring of the Holy Spirit whereby there is no division between secular and religious knowledge.

Charlotte Mason's expressed wish was that although she should not be remembered yet the work she did for the children's sake should continue. Her college in Ambleside still bears her name but no longer are teachers trained to carry out her theories. Her schools no longer practice her methods or follow her curriculum. In the name of modernization all has changed. Change is not always for the better and some reappraisal of her philosophy may hold the answer to some of the present problems.

Part One Section Two

The First Principle

Children are born *persons*.

Children come into the world as complete persons. The tiny baby and the grown man are equal in this respect. The differences between adult and child depend on what has happened in the intervening years.

To spoil a child is not just to give way to his every whim; it is literally to damage his personality. This can be done in many ways. Charlotte Mason summed them up under the headings 'Offending the Children'. 'Despising the Children' and 'Hindering the Children'. Parents and teachers would not wilfully do any of these things to children but it will be seen how unconsciously children can be offended, despised, and hindered. Children should be treated with respect even if they seem to abuse the confidence we put in them as persons.

What is a child in society? 'A tablet to be written upon?' 'A twig to be bent? Wax to be moulded? He may be all this but he is much more.' It was once said of children 'Of such is the Kingdom of Heaven,' and of grown men, 'Except ye become as little children ye shall in no case enter the Kingdom of Heaven.' 'Who is the greatest in the Kingdom?' they asked. And He set a little child in their midst. There is no doubt that Christ recognized the spirituality of children and that there are ways in which it can be destroyed. This presupposes a Christian ethic which Charlotte Mason would be the first to acknowledge. The point for our purposes is that her theory works in practice. Can as much be said for many of the so-called progressive theories of the present day educational sociologists?

Charlotte Mason's philosophy of education has proved to be successful with children from every walk of life, the able and the less able, and, because of its catholicity, children of all nations and creeds.

The present educational debate concerns itself with curricula and grouping of children, with facilities and costs, staffing ratios and counselling. How often is the child considered as a person in society, as a spiritual being having a close relationship with a Heavenly Father? The children ask for bread and society gives them a stone.

'If we let the people sink into the mire of a material education our doom is sealed, eyes now living will see us take even a third-rate place among the nations.' Was Charlotte Mason a prophet?

How then is a child offended? When a stumbling-block is placed in his path, by the inconsistency of parents and teachers, when what is right and allowed one day becomes wrong and forbidden the next. How can the child be sure of the law when 'the law is an ass'? Soon the child begins to choose for himself what he will do or not do. In the tiny child it may seem to amuse or it may be said that the child is a determined young person who already knows his own mind or is showing a grand independence of character. Children grow and their demands grow with them unless their natural capacity for co-operation is fostered by wise control and consistent regulation. This is particularly important for the child of today, when so much is insecure, to know from the start what is or is not permissible gives a child a sense of purpose. If a child is to learn right from wrong he must see in the lives of those who surround him the same respect for right and wrong.

Why should it be permissible for the grown-up to be untruthful or unkind, to use bad language or to cheat, when these are the actions not allowed the younger persons in the family? Surely for the child to believe that to be grown-up means to be able to please oneself in every matter is one of the biggest stumbling-blocks in the way of his proper development.

The child who is accepted as a person will find an outlet for his emotions in the family circle and the wonder of the universe. A whole life can be marred by the stumbling-block of coldness and lack of interest which meets the outpouring of a loving nature.

Intellectually a child's development will be stultified by lack of progress or achievement. The young mind moves fast and is ready for new things once one stage has been reached. Even the dull child will respond to praise and encouragement and the satisfaction of knowing that progress is being made. How many a stumbling-block is put in the path of the gifted child because he can move faster than his contemporaries? To be held back is just as frustrating as to be given tasks beyond one's capabilities. The child as a person must not be offended in these matters.

To despise is to undervalue. How often are children rebuffed by an adult who undervalues their contribution to society. Who has no time to listen or to look, no time for companionship and sharing experiences? The grown-up world is too busy and the children's thoughts are brushed aside as trivial. To this age which fosters egalitarianism Charlotte Mason would reiterate to parents and teachers what Christ said to those who tried to silence the children: 'If these should be silent, the very stones would cry out.'

It is so easy to suggest a better time for some long tale and the child needs to learn to bide awhile. If the matter is important but not urgent the child who has learnt to take his proper place in society will be patient if he knows the grown-ups can be trusted to keep their word. In letting the children down even in little things we are despising them.

Charlotte Mason knew nothing of television so we can only surmise how she would value 'the box'. It would be valued for what can be learnt not only for entertainment. Children should be expected to express in some way what they had seen and encouraged to discover or do things for themselves. The serialized classics which are so popular should be read first so that the children can exercise their imaginations and make their own mental pictures before they are indoctrinated by someone else's. To use the television just to keep the children quiet is a way of undervaluing them. Charlotte Mason would have been saddened to see so many children unable to express themselves in good clear language which can only be achieved by reading or being read to. Language is a very important aspect of society and a part of culture which is sadly neglected. Conversation is a lost art and apparently no longer part of family relationships, when children no longer sit round the table for a family meal but live a snack-snatching kind of life. This is not good enough for the children of the nation, her most precious possession. Nothing but the best of ourselves is good enough for them.

The third precept: Do not hinder!

Charlotte Mason died in 1923 when the world was hardly divesting itself of the blemishes of war and when men's minds were still filled with the hope of a new society, fit for heroes. Disillusionment was just round the corner. The gay abandonment of the 1920s was a cover-up for the deep-seated fears which lay below the surface. The Nazi Party had already been founded in Germany, and in the same month when Charlotte Mason died the U.S.S.R. was established. Women had taken their place in Parliament. They flattened their chests, and provocatively smoked cigarettes in long holders. The old values were being thrown overboard and the existence of God was questioned.

What of the children as the rot set in and society began to fall apart? How were they hindered?

Charlotte Mason held that it is in the nature of a child to have a spiritual relationship with God. By our agnosticism we stand in the way of this relationship. Fifty years, another war, and still we come between the children and God. The child learns to love God through living in a family. When the family disintegrates the child loses more than physical security. He loses the ability to make relationships and the reflection of his bond with God which he saw in the family becomes blurred. This is how we hinder the children.

If parents have no faith of their own or have lost the faith they had, how can they do otherwise than hinder the children? 'Let the children find out for themselves' is not good enough and it puts a doubt in their minds from the very start. When we look at the sad state of the world today, fifty years since Charlotte Mason reminded her readers of Christ's command to His disciples 'Suffer little children to come unto me and forbid them not', we can see where society has taken the wrong road.

As the power of gravity holds the universe in place so man's soul is held in the palm of God's hand. Woe to them that hinder the operation of God's will. By disbelief God is not displaced. But the proper development of the child is hindered. It is a child's birthright that he be brought to know God.

Perhaps we can now see a little more clearly what Charlotte Mason meant when she said 'Children are born persons. They are not born good or bad, but with possibilities for good and evil.' There is no greater service to the nation than for the parents and teachers to face the implications of Charlotte Mason's first principle that children are born persons and to put them in the way of achieving the maximum which lies within their personality.

Part One Section Three

The Second Principle

'Authority on the one hand and Docility on the other are natural, necessary and fundamental.'

We hear much criticism of authoritarian methods of teaching and much praise of equality. Charlotte Mason would agree that authoritarian attitudes towards children are at fault because they suggest that the child is an inferior being. Equality to Charlotte Mason meant a sharing of knowledge and experiences between the teacher and the taught on the basis of the mutual respect the one should have for the other.

When a child realizes that parents and teachers are themselves under authority and that they must do what they ought to do, then a fundamental principle is established and the child becomes teachable.

Charlotte Mason likened Authority and Docility to the way in which the force of gravity holds the universe in order. Without these two principles there can be no order in society. If authority is too rigid on the one hand or teachableness lacking on the other the result is chaos. Likewise a lack of authority or a submissive child is calamitous. Time has proved her to be right. In trying to liberate the children by creating a permissive society we have baffled the children with insecurity.

B

What is true of the physical world of behaviour is also true of the mental world. When a certain person is said to be an authority on a particular subject we know his knowledge has been gained by painstaking study and disciplined thinking. This cannot be achieved in any other way. So too the teacher and the child must similarly apply themselves if any standard but the lowest is to be arrived at. We value most those things for which we have striven, thus the knowledge obtained through a disciplined application of the mind is the knowledge we value and care about.

Children as persons require this schooling if they are to achieve their own individual potential. They thrive on the effort required to do the thing which is difficult. without this stimulation they soon become bored and 'careless'. The teacher is there to guide and particularly to encourage. Prizes, marks and awards are not necessary; the work itself is sufficient fulfilment. To know that a truth has been arrived at gives not only confidence to the searcher but also delight.

To quote Charlotte Mason's own words clarifies her thoughts on authority and docility.

'Docility implies equality: there is no great gulf fixed between teacher and taught; both are pursuing the same ends, engaged on the same theme, enriched by mutual interests, and probably the quite delightful pursuit of knowledge affords the only intrinsic liberty for both teacher and taught.'

Charlotte Mason was not only a theorist. Through her own experience as a teacher and her contacts with others engaged in the same profession she was always ready with practical advice for parents and teachers on the 'shop floor' of education. To secure teachableness and obedience in home and classroom there must be two conditions in evidence. *One*: regulations must not be for the convenience of the teacher nor should they be arbitrary. Although the taken-for-granted ideology of her day no longer holds sway in our permissive society, we may however learn a lesson from this state of affairs which will help us to return to a road from which we have diverged. When docility and authority went out of fashion in homes and schools disorder ensued.

The second condition is, in Charlotte Mason's words:

'That children should have a fine sense of the freedom which comes of knowledge which they are allowed to appropriate as they choose.' The matter to be studied must be presented in literary form, not watered down or oft-repeated. The mind as also the body requires good nourishing food, not predigested slops. 'Hungry minds of children will absorb it, assimilate it and grow by it.' The choice comes naturally. What they are unable to digest will be rejected. Read Bunyan's *Pilgrim's Progress* or Lewis Carroll's *Alice in Wonderland* to eight or nine-year-olds and read them again when adult and what Charlotte Mason meant by freedom to choose will be apparent. Surely this is why we never tire of the best in literature. As we grow so it comes to mean more to us.

It is interesting to re-read Charlotte Mason's books, for though one might imagine she lived a life sheltered from the stresses and strains of modern life she was well aware of the problems facing parents and teachers of all times. We have come to accept disorderly and unruly children and young adults who go about creating havoc and distress. Describing the young in her day she wrote: 'They are devoid of intellectual interests, history and poetry are without charm for them, the scientific work of the day is only slightly interesting, their "job" and the social amenities they can secure are all that their life has for them.' This she calls a maimed existence in exchange for which she offers an education and a way of life that is as necessary today as it was when she was writing at the beginning of the century.

We know that there are many splendid young people who are preparing to take their places in society as responsible citizens. We are also aware of the growing crime rate among other youngsters. Obviously their upbringing has not been successful. Could it be that we are on the wrong road and a return to some of the values of the past would bode well for the future?

Part One Section Four

The Family

The family as a unit played an important part in Charlotte Mason's philosophy. It is in the family that real socialism is to be found, not the socialism of everyone for himself but the socialism of equal sharing of whatever is available. The family unit begins to break up when the individuals demand more than their rightful share, be it of love, or privilege, or goods; in fact when greed and envy find their way into the community.

This is as true of nations as of families, which are the basis of the nation. The social history of our times will be founded on the effect broken families have on the nation as a whole. Never has so much needed to be done for men, women and children in the form of social services for those whose lives are marred by the break-up of their families.

It is within the family circle which includes several generations and also courtesy 'aunts and uncles' that the young learn by example, consideration for others, manners, kindness, generosity, unselfishness, and a host of other graces which, if not learnt at home, are never so much part of a person but a veneer that easily loses its lustre.

'The restoration of the family is a labour that unites

us here in England, for there is little doubt that the family bond is more lax amongst us than it was two or three generations ago,' wrote Charlotte Mason at the beginning of this century. Family ties have continued to loosen until we now ask ourselves whether the family matters at all. Is it just an inherited idea that those outside the family are better qualified to train the young?

Those who bring new lives into the world have the greatest responsibility in the whole nation placed upon them. Fathers are more important than Prime Ministers, and mothers than social workers, for they are the governors and the preservers of the family. Their individual positions are of vital importance to the peace of the family and the ordering of the nation.

Those who operate the family planning and marriage guidance organizations should receive every kind of support. Above all the churches should lead the way to a better understanding of the power of parents to make or mar the lives of children committed to their care.

Charlotte Mason insisted that no one can deputize for a parent, and no parent should abdicate from the position of authority invested in him by God. Parental authority is to be used for the well-being of the children and through them for service to the nation. At the same time parents must bear in mind that a single decision made by them, which the child is, or should be, capable of making for himself, is an encroachment on the rights of the child. Within this balance between autocracy and human rights not only will the family be secure but the nation will be blessed with peaceful government. Political parties, families and institutions might all learn a lesson from Charlotte Mason who said:

'The highest art lies in ruling without seeming to do so – happy is the household that has few rules.'

Part One Section Five

The Sanctity of Personality

With the principles of authority and docility in mind, Charlotte Mason would have us aware of the power we have over children, and of thoughts which lead us to think we have a right to do what we will with our own.

Two of the strongest powers we can exert over children are fear and love. There was a time when children were brought under control by fear. They feared the punishments meted out to them for the smallest misdemeanours, and they feared those under whose authority they dwelt either at home or at school. When we think how easy-going the modern adults are with children we wonder that the children of earlier generations ever survived. Mutual respect between young and adult precludes the use of fear as a means of obtaining obedience and co-operation. The educator is to lead in the right direction by encouragement and example. If the child needs punishment in order to emphasize correction then the punishment must be quickly administered and soon forgotten. It must not only fit the crime but also the child. Charlotte Mason would have said that corporal punishment is degrading for both parties and if it seems necessary it is because of failure not only on the part of the child to realize that obedience is necessary for safety and for the general good order of life, but also on the part of the adult because of a lack of understanding of how to achieve a right relationship between authority and docility.

To exploit the affections of children is equally destructive of the very relationship adults ought to be fostering. 'Daddy won't love you any more,' is an unpardonable expression. Just as devastating for the child is the adult who tries to test a child's love by using it as a bribe to obtain obedience. "If you really loved me, you would do as I say." This use of affection is one of the quickest ways to destroy love. It is not the way we should try to obtain loyalty and co-operation. Whatever they do the children must always feel loved by their parents and respected by their teachers.

The use of suggestion is another way in which adults can use their power wrongly. A child will learn to do what he is asked to do, if the request is reasonable and the time and place convenient. To give freedom of choice and then suggest the right choice is to give the child no freedom of choice at all. Choices are very difficult for children and are best limited to one or two alternatives. Gradually the child learns to stand on his own feet and make considered choices about all manner of things. Sometimes suggestion can so influence the child that quite the wrong career is embarked upon. Children are so malleable that undue influence brought upon them can stultify the development of personality to such an extent that when they become adult they are still unable to make their own independent decisions. We all know the grown woman who can't go shopping without her mother, or the man who fails in business because he has no confidence in himself to make the right decision at the opportune moment.

Within the child himself there are natural desires which can be played upon to achieve the ambitions of parents and teachers. The natural desire for approbation can be wrongly stimulated by prizes and awards so that the child thinks more of them than of what they stand for. To do well in school to please those he loves, and who care for him, is laudable, so long as the effort, perseverance, and skill required are also recognized as praiseworthy. There are children who never make the top grade but whose characters are formed by the determination required just to keep pace.

The society in which children will eventually find themselves is very competitive and many fall by the wayside, because too much emphasis is placed on winning and not enough on the means employed. Cramming to gain a scholarship, training to get into a team may be good in some ways and perhaps necessary on occasion but Charlotte Mason would have us watch that the natural desire for knowledge is not stillborn in the child or the joy of the out-of-doors or physical activity not lost, by undue emphasis on competition.

The desire for power over others is very strong in some children, who at a very early age become leaders or organizers of gangs or teams. This desire must be trained so that it is used for the benefit of the group as a whole and not for the aggrandisement of the individual or at the expense of the less strong personalities. One of the strongest desires inherent in humanity is the desire for knowledge. Charlotte Mason was very insistent that knowledge of all kinds should be made available to children. Knowledge is not the prerogative of the adult world and the freedom to know must be available for the proper development of mind in the same way as food is made available for the body.

We are inclined to provide a variety of predigested slops, or watered-down, made-easy information. Nothing could be better guaranteed to bore and spoil the appetite of the child for real knowledge, described by Charlotte Mason as information touched with emotion. To know is to care about, and to desire to know more, to explore and discover.

Charlotte Mason would have said to those modern theorists who preach child-centred curricula and progressive methods, 'Remember to provide nourishment for the child's mind that he can bite and chew on and there will develop a mind that has something to grow on.' If the soil is rich the roots will penetrate it and find what they need to produce flower and fruit. Even so the child's appetite can only be satisfied by a diet of real knowledge, as contained in books which have not been rewritten for children. Explanations, unless asked for, are tedious and what is not understood will be passed over, but not necessarily forgotten. It may be that at some later date the concept which has not been grasped will fall into place as so often happens with jigsaw puzzles.

Part One Section Six

Masterly Inactivity

One of Charlotte Mason's ideas which she strongly impressed on her students was what she called 'masterly inactivity' — excellent in theory but very hard to practise.

The mother cat will let her kittens venture on their own but she is ever at hand to rescue them from harm, and to show them how to conduct their lives. So too with children. 'Let them be,' said Charlotte Mason. 'Nature will look after him and give him promptings of desire to KNOW many things, and somebody must tell as he wants to know, and TO DO many things, and somebody should be handy just to put him in the way, and TO BE many things, and somebody should give direction.' *Home Education* p.192, C.M. Mason

Is the modern child pushed around, analysed, urged, pressed into activities, surrounded by choices, to such an extent that there is no time to push down roots and to grow? As soon as the opportunity to throw off the shackles presents itself they are away and gone to some place where they are free, free to find themselves.

The inactivity which Charlotte Mason talked about was not heedlessness. On the contrary it was masterly.

The parent or teacher must always be in control of any situation and ready to help when help is asked for.

We all know how tempting it is to build with the child's bricks, to decide which story to read, to plan the future. To stand back and watch a young person disregard advice is perhaps one of the most difficult lessons the adults have to learn. But children who are regarded as persons from the day they are born, who have shared what is available on equal terms and who know that there is always someone to turn to in time of need are less likely to kick over the traces and make serious mistakes. They will not leave the shelter of home until they know themselves to be adequate for life in the outside world.

In the classroom where the teacher's voice is heard delivering a lecture, dictating notes, asking questions, the pupils are not given any time to think for themselves. It is what the teacher thinks the child should know which is going in at one ear and out of the other. The human mind must be given time to read, mark, learn and inwardly digest before there is any sign of understanding and this can only be tested by the pupil himself relating what he knows.

Give a dog a marrow bone and he will wrestle with it till all the goodness has been absorbed. Give the children living ideas in well-written books and they will grapple with the contents and make them their own.

Masterly inactivity is hard to achieve because the grown-ups are so anxious for the children to have everything and miss nothing. They are dragged through stately homes and shewn everything when they might have gained more simply by looking at the view from one of the windows or being allowed to linger over *one* picture that attracted their attention. A book full of pictures is often less appreciated than a story well written which allows you to make your own pictures. Television is quite the reverse of masterly inactivity because it gives the children the pictures grown-ups have chosen and leaves no scope for imagination. It is better to play 'let's pretend' games than always to be entertained by 'the box'.

Children will make mistakes, they will misbehave in all manner of ways. This is the natural way to grow up. The child who is too securely guarded against his mistakes has little chance of learning by experience. Masterly inactivity exercised by parents and teachers is at hand to prevent serious damage and to 'pick up the bits' and renew confidence when all seems lost.

Part One Section Seven

Three Instruments of Education

We have dealt with powers we may not use in the education of our children. And perhaps we are left with a feeling of inadequacy for the task. We may not use the power that love or fear have over the child to coerce him into obedience or mental effort. We may not use awards and prizes to stimulate his desire for emulation. We may only use his desire for knowledge which Charlotte Mason maintains is sufficient to draw out from a child all the effort and perseverance necessary for his proper education.

There are three instruments which are available to parents and teachers. Atmosphere, Discipline and Life are the three positive instruments to be employed in the home and the school. Home is the most important environment but teachers and parents must work together. If there is friction between them the child is subjected to a conflict of loyalties. Therefore parents have the greater responsibility for their children's upbringing.

Atmosphere

Charlotte Mason was not in favour of the creation of a special environment for children. White tiles and carpeted floors do not make a good school, neither is the well-to-do home where there is little love better than the rough and tumble of a large working class family where there is affection and sharing of what is available. Many of our great men grew up in straitened circumstances. No — atmosphere is more subtle than environment. We have learnt by the bitter experience of vandalism in modern housing estates and wanton destruction of school property that the physical environment is not the strongest influence in the lives of children. It is the atmosphere of respect and understanding created in the home where the child knows he is wanted and the classroom where he can do what he is able to do.

Again Charlotte Mason uses the analogy of the plant to emphasize her theory. The greenhouse plant must be protected all its life; one blast of cold air and it withers. The plant that grows exposed to all weathers in its natural clime develops a form of protection which sustains life. This does not mean that no effort should be made to look after the soil or provide moisture in times of drought. To create the right atmosphere we must consider again Charlotte Mason's insistence on the child as a person and not, as can be the case, a pawn in the lives of adults to be pushed around according to whim or inclination.

Play groups and nursery schools have their place in modern life to accommodate to the many changes that have taken place since Charlotte Mason's day. It would be fair to say that she would look upon them as necessary for the modern mothers who either go out to work or who need some relief from their children because so many of them come from small families and have themselves little experience of domesticity. The danger is that a special environment is created for the children which has little resemblance to their natural surroundings and this can cause confusion and stress in the child. It is the attitude of the adults to the children which creates the atmosphere in which they can respond and have room to grow. To Charlotte Mason they were children or boys and girls, not 'kids', 'kiddies', or 'brats'. This may seem a little thing but it could be indicative of the way we think of them.

Discipline

The second instrument available to educators is the discipline of habit. We all know the strength of a habit and how difficult it is to break a bad one or to form a good one, yet habit is a great aid to education. Once formed the habit of writing legibly is always with us so long as we exercise it. There are a hundred and one things we do by habit every day. The way we dress ourselves, the way we hold a knife and fork, the very act of walking — the list is endless. All these conditioned reflexes had to be formed by the habitual use of the same nerves and muscles. Habits of thinking do a great deal to build up the person. We form our opinions by thinking along the same lines over and over again.

Charlotte Mason expressed the power of habit as being ten times as strong as nature. By nature she meant the natural desires, appetites, affections common to all humans, the sum total of which is called 'human nature'. Every society has its conventions and rules, children must not be left to the devices of human nature but directed along channels of activity by the force of habit. This is not a contradiction to the theory of letting them be but a way of easing their lives so that their attention may be taken up with interesting pursuits and achievement.

The habit of paying attention to instructions is a

case in point. Give simple instructions (one at a time to little children) and ask them to repeat what you have said before they dash off heedless of your intentions.

The habit of sitting and standing correctly can relieve stress in later years. The habit of reading for pleasure can begin before the skill of reading is mastered, if only someone will read to the children instead of just sitting them in front of the television. The habit of consideration for others is learnt from example as are so many of the graces. This is the area in which we fail our children. We do not insist on the formation of good habits from the very start of life and we so often set a bad example ourselves.

Certain habits can be cultivated in the classroom to bring about the smooth running of the day leaving time for learning and for the delight in knowledge. It is however particularly in the home that the instrument of habit can be seen as an aid to education.

Take for example bedtime. If it is always at a certain time, except for special occasions, then there is no argument. Some may be surprised to find that most children thrive on an orderly routine and dislike a change of regime. It may appear monotonous but it does provide a background of security and a relief from having to make choices.

Charlotte Mason speaks of habits to be formed in every field of the children's lives: cleanliness, obedience, truthfulness, attention to detail. With this theory put into practice not only will human nature be trained, but also inherited traits can be brought under control, whether they are good or bad. Generosity can be as damaging to a person as selfishness. The too generous needs to learn to curb his desire to give away if it ends in making him a burden to his neighbours, the selfish to form a habit of sharing with others what he does not need for himself.

So the formation of habits can be a liberating force in the life of the growing child, and in no way does it restrict the development of personality. Rather it makes it possible for him to make more of himself.

Life

The third instrument of education is life.

Charlotte Mason asks us to look upon the child's mind as a spiritual organism. It is alive and in need of nourishment just as is the physical body. Ideas are the natural diet of the mind. An idea 'strikes' the mind and is absorbed. It then begins to behave like a living cell in the physical body. By thought processes it grows and nourishes the mind. One idea leads to another and so minds make contact with one another. In saying that education is life Charlotte Mason is referring to the living ideas expressed in great works of art, music, and literature and in scientific progress in many fields. For children to effect any satisfactory relationship between their minds and the minds of great men and women they must be brought into direct contact through their works.

'The only fit sustenance for the mind is ideas. An idea, like the single cell of cellular tissue, appears to go through the stages and functions of a life.'

When a child's mind is nourished in this way he becomes knowledgeable, that is, he is put in the way of experiencing what he learns. The faculties of reason, imagination, reflection, and judgement are brought to bear on the matter in hand which becomes part of the life of the child. If these faculties are not stultified by a diet of predigested information and illustrations which leave no scope for the imagination, or the cramming of facts which allow no time for reflection, or reveal the prejudices of the teacher, then the mind of the child will blossom and the intellect flourish.

Men have spoken of the liberty of the individual conscience and have forgotten that there is such a thing as the liberty of the individual mind to choose or disregard the knowledge provided. Unless it is presented in the form of living ideas most of it will be disregarded.

I have known a group of children aged between 8 and 10 discuss and compare the works of great painters with a perception and sagacity equal to students twice their age, simply because they had been given the opportunity to look at and into pictures, to reflect on them and to perceive the ideas of the painter expressed in his work.

Part Two Section One

Curriculum

'Few things are more remiss in our schools than the curriculum which is supposed to be entirely at the option of the Head: but is it? Most secondary schools work towards examinations which more or less afford the privilege of entry to Universities. The standard to be reached is set by these and the Heads of schools hold themselves powerless.'

If this was true when Charlotte Mason wrote it, it is more true today. A system of options operates at secondary level and subjects which are not studied for examination purposes are dropped or regarded as non-essential, so we can have a situation where boys and girls of thirteen and fourteen study no History, Geography and very little Literature. Art, Crafts and Music are time-fillers for the less able. Examination pressure precludes many youngsters from enjoying purposeful leisure activities, either because they have no time to spare from examination work or because long hours spent in travelling and in home study sap their energies to such an extent that when freed from school, they turn to disrupting the life of others, their pent-up physical energies exploding in acts of violence and vandalism. Instead of training the children to use their minds we try to cram into them a mass of useless information so that they can pass examinations. Pass they do — perhaps — but they don't know or care to know.

'Education is the Science of Relations — our business is not to teach him all about anything, but to help him to make valid as many as may be of —

"Those first-born affinities that fit our new existence to existing things".'

So we have three areas where the existing relationship must needs be fostered and enlarged.

1) Knowledge of God,
2) Knowledge of the Universe, and
3) Knowledge of Man.

Knowledge of God can best be 'taught' in the home where the family life can be a reflection of the larger family incorporating all mankind. Caring for one another in the small family unit can grow into a caring for those outside the family. Children learn best how to pray when prayer is part of everyday family life, so too with a knowledge of the Scriptures.

All this may seem remote from the modern way of life, old-fashioned and irrelevant. The point being that a relationship exists between a child and God which needs to be fostered and enlarged. The fact that in modern times this relationship has been destroyed or neglected does not prove that it does not exist or that we should not be the better for it. Charlotte Mason regarded the family as the basis of national strength. If this is true everything possible should be done to repair the damage already done to society by the breakdown of family life and to inculcate in young people the responsibilities inherent in parenthood.

What is begun at home can be continued in school

by a close and consistent study of Scripture — both Old and New Testaments — so that the unfolding of God's purposes in the life of Christ can be a lively experience in the children's minds. The whole story from Genesis to Revelation is peopled with men and women like themselves, with the same weaknesses and the same strengths. Surely there is no better way to understanding one another than a knowledge of men and women of the past.

This leads us to consider the second area of the curriculum — Knowledge of Man — History, Citizenship, Geography, Literature, Language, Art, Music, and Craftsmanship. History should cover the story of mankind from his first appearance on the planet to the present day. This general history as paralleled by the history of our own nation. Citizenship opens the mind to biography and forms of government. Regional Geography with its attendant physical geography helps in the understanding of other nations and our interdependence on one another, and Relationships in every direction.

Literature and the study of Language are not only for enjoyment of the story but help to develop the means of communication between people, another aspect of relationships. Art and Music through which the aesthetic sense is developed is not only valuable to the would-be artist or musician but an aid to the appreciation of what has been done by great masters. Stately homes and museums come alive when those whose work we know and love can be recognized and understood.

Knowledge of the Universe is the third and last area to be included in the curriculum of all children of school age. No one nowadays would consider any curriculum adequate which did not include the sciences. When Charlotte Mason wrote her *Essay Towards a Philosophy of Education*, first published in 1925, the sciences were only just being made available to all children under the 'umbrella' of a liberal education for all. However, even then she was able to write:

'As a matter of fact the teaching of science in our schools has lost much of its *educative* value through a fatal and quite unnecessary divorce between science and the "humanities".'

Science has become a utilitarian subject and so lost much of its educative value, particularly for the unscientific children who can nevertheless appreciate the wonder and beauty of much that a knowledge of the universe affords. No knowledge of the universe is complete without Mathematics and in this area untold stumbling-blocks have been put in the way of children, because we have created such a mountain of mathematics that the way to many careers is blocked to all who are unable to surmount its problems, which become more obscure and irrelevant for each generation. Exactitude and precision of thought can be developed through other areas of the curriculum. Turning again to Charlotte Mason's very words, which we would be wise to consider:

'Mathematics are a necessary part of every man's education; they must be taught by those who know; but they may not engross the time and attention of the scholar in such wise as to shut out any of the score of "subjects", a knowledge of which is his natural right.'

In the Great Educational Debate we have heard much of 'core' curricula, options, specialization, school subjects related to adult skills, etc., but very little has been said about knowledge and the satisfaction of knowing rather than being informed: The delight children experience when they discover something that their studies have lead them towards, and the spiritual and moral value of disciplined learning which alone can form the foundation of a liberal education. We are beginning to discover the potential of the handicapped child. How many children are being handicapped through a narrowing of the curriculum at an early age?

Part Two — Section Two

Syllabi

In the debate which concerns itself with the curriculum Charlotte Mason believed that the only right road is wide with many minor roads joining the main stream of traffic. Children have a right to knowledge as they are able to absorb it and it must be presented in good literary form. Books, books and more books which the children handle and read themselves. They are not to be reduced to a diet of rehashes, lectures and notes produced by the teacher. They must learn by degrees to select what is of interest and of vital importance, for themselves. Only thus will they be able to sift and discover the information they need in any particular situation. The use of libraries and encyclopedias should be part of their discipline. Lessons should stimulate a desire to know more and the ability to research the knowledge they desire.

Syllabi will be in the hands of heads of departments or examining boards which must perforce narrow the scope of study. The years leading up to preparation for public examinations can take a wider view of the various subjects. This wide foundation will give stability and understanding upon which further study can be built.

Integration was not in any way special to Charlotte Mason. What better way of understanding history is there than to have a knowledge of contemporary literature? The study of the history of other countries and the social development of differing regions is helped by geography. Children should be introduced to the idea of the wholeness of knowledge, which should never be divided into segregated departments. Music and art are cosmopolitan, genius is not the prerogative of any race or nation. All this makes a nonsense of subject divisions which so often limit children to areas of knowledge in which they can shine. The proper education of the responsible citizen must be magnanimous.

History then must include ancient history, foreign history as it relates to the history of one's own country. Citizenship, (a knowledge of government and of men and women who have contributed most to society), linked to literature and languages. Chronology can be illustrated by time-lines and charts built up by the children. Completing a century by filling in one inch squares on a large sheet of paper can be a fascinating occupation and when completed the history of a whole century can be grasped at a glance. There is no shortage of authors of historical novels and here the modern child has television also to aid his imagination. Charlotte Mason was enthusiastic about visits to places of historical interest but the children must be informed visitors to such places to reap any benefit. If a lasting impression is to be gained, such visits must be reported on, not with the endless quiz sheets but the child's own record of what attracts his attention. While he is busy answering someone else's questions he is not asking his own.

Geography is in both the humanities and the science camps. It bridges the disciplines and while regional geography covers the living conditions of the whole world, physical and geological studies give a reasoned account of those conditions. How poor is the education of the child who has dropped geography, particularly at a time when travel and the media draw us all closer together in a physical sense. Would a more comprehensive knowledge of geography make us more ready to live at peace with one another? Or how can one begin to understand economics without some basic geographical knowledge?

If literature and history are inseparable so too are literature and language. Latin and Greek have fallen by the wayside and are not taught at all in some schools. Small wonder that an understanding of syntax is lacking in written language. Foreign languages should find a place in every curriculum. No knowledge stands alone, all knowledge helps to nourish the mind and build up the person into a whole being.

Every scientist must be a trained observer and Charlotte Mason would have us train the children in powers of observation, not only through actual science lessons but in all aspects of life. The habit of noticing little details in everyday situations and particularly when out of doors, by sea or countryside, and keeping records of plant and animal life is part of the basic training for a scientific career. Charlotte Mason left no avenue unexplored if she felt it could contribute to the children's delight in knowledge. 'We are educated by our intimacies' was one of her firm beliefs. Children's enthusiasms go through many changes but they provide wonderful opportunities for the teacher, who must be flexible enough to use them.

In 1893 Charlotte Mason visited Florence in order to regain her health. While on this visit, accompanied by Mrs Firth whose daughter Julia was a friend of Ruskin's, she visited the Spanish Chapel attached to the Church of Santa Maria Novella and saw the fresco depicting the descent of the Holy Spirit upon men's minds. This made a deep impression on Charlotte Mason and she called it 'The Great Recognition'. From the outpouring of the Holy Spirit comes the enlightenment of mankind. Herein lies the kernel of her philosphy. Every aspect of education which has this illuminating idea within it will be alive with potency.

The teacher or parent with this thought in mind becomes the vessel of knowledge and not the provider. The child in his care is no longer one of many, but the one whose relationships with all that is known must be allowed freedom to grow.

In the next section Charlotte Mason's method of teaching will be explained and this will allay the fears of those readers who may be wondering how all this can be encompassed in the short time allocated to schooling.

Part Two Section Three

Method

How is all this accomplished?

Charlotte Mason planned the school day so that lessons in academic subjects took up the morning, leaving the afternoon for physical education, creative work in art and other practical activities. The evenings were left for purposeful leisure and particularly reading. (There was no television in her day, and even the radio was limited in its scope.)

In the modern school day it is not possible to organize the time table in this way but certain fundamental principles can be borne in mind. The most demanding work in any subject can be done in the morning. Some physical activity should be included every day with some time spent out of doors. Homework should not be so demanding as to preclude the enjoyment of leisure activities or participation in youth clubs of various kinds. This would be possible if more work were done during the school day. By this I mean less note taking and more learning.

Here an explanation of the method of learning advocated by Charlotte Mason is called for.

1) Each lesson begins with some form of recapitulation of the previous lesson.

2) The day's lesson is then introduced, names, dates,

pictures and difficult words learnt.

3) A passage is read aloud preferably by the pupils. (It is a sad commentary on modern teaching that so few children read aloud well.)

4) The passage must be long enough to capture the interest of the pupils and to hold their attention, leaving them with an appetite for more.

5) This passage is then retold by one or more pupils, beginning at the beginning and following the whole sequence of the argument. No corrections or interruptions are allowed during this narration. The passage is never reread.

6) The teacher then draws *from the class* any necessary corrections or emphasis of important facts through discussion and question.

Variety can be brought in by group work, written narration of part of the lesson, dramatic representation or illustration, particularly with young children. Older children write their own summaries picking out salient facts from a paragraph or section of reading without referring to the book. This applies to all written work. When pupils know that only one reading is allowed, their powers of concentration are not dissipated. The following benefits emerge from this method:

1) A great deal of ground is covered.

2) No time is wasted. (The pupils ask the questions.)

3) Every pupil is involved either as a reader or in narration and the correction of narrations which may be necessary. Learning is a shared experience.

4) The pupils learn to express themselves in fluent spoken language or in good written work.

5) Spelling and punctuation become the norm through the handling of well-written living litera-

ture which is absolutely necessary if this method of learning is to be successful.

6) Revision is unnecessary and undesirable. The pupils are tested at the end of each term, during one week, when they write answers to questions which are so worded as to recall that which has been absorbed by them, because it was interesting and made relevant through discussion. What they know is the important factor.

7) The best written results are obtained if the work can be done in class immediately after the reading, while the ideas are fresh in the mind and before any questions are raised.

8) Science subjects and mathematics can be treated in much the same way. A mind trained by this method brings powers of concentration and accuracy of thought to bear on any matter to be studied.

The use of this method presupposes that the teacher has prepared the lessons and used her skill to bring variety into each day's work. There should always be an element of surprise in every lesson. Only an occasional oral lecture need be given. If the right books are used the pupils are keen to get on with the next passage and their narrations are eagerly shared among them. *They* do the work in class if the teachers have done theirs beforehand.

Written work must be corrected but with a well planned day this can be spread over the week. There are ways of minimizing this part of a teacher's responsibility and if piles of books are taken home each evening, the teacher must be managing badly.

One hears much of class indiscipline in these days. Perhaps we should look to our methods and to the books we use, the time and care spent in preparation and correction of work, before we condemn the modern child. Surely the adults, parents and teachers and society as a whole are to blame if the children no longer want to know about the world they live in, are bored or intractable. Of course the deprived (rich or poor) child will find learning difficult because his mind is not free from stresses and society. While we busy ourselves with wondering what is wrong with our modern young we forget that greed and selfishness among adults are possibly the root of the trouble. Charlotte Mason gave her teachers a simple motto as their guiding thought in all their work:

'For The Children's Sake'

One word must be said about the size of class. Any satisfactory rapport between teacher and taught is hard to achieve with classes as large as 30 to 40 pupils. How many individuals do other adults outside the teaching profession have to deal with in their work? Some way must be found to reduce the size of class.

The adult literacy campaign is staffed to a large extent by voluntary workers. Why not voluntary workers in the classroom? Many retired teachers or experts in various fields could use their skills to relieve the overburdened teacher of a large class. Voluntary helpers are working in every other field of social work. Surely work in the classroom need not be monopolized by the professionals?

The teacher who knows her pupils, knows who to choose for the difficult passages, whose written work is better than his oral work, who is best at recapitulation and who needs encouragement by being given the short paragraphs to read or descriptive passages to narrate.

The teacher must draw the attention of her class to the beginning of each passage or she may find that no one can begin to narrate although the middle and end of the passage are well retold. Without asking direct questions a teacher can start the ball rolling.

Some major facts must be memorized and every day should have a time for memory work. Ten to fifteen minutes a day spent in learning poetry will develop the ability to memorize not only history dates and literature, prose as well as poetry, and foreign languages, but also formulae in science and multiplication tables. Many senior citizens tell us of the value of a well-stored memory as faculties for learning new things become weakened.

Charlotte Mason was probably the first educationalist to advocate visits to museums, galleries, concerts and other educational journeys, provided the children know about the things they are seeing or hearing and are free to relate their own impressions after the visit. The questionnaires one sees being completed by children these days certainly keep them busy and reasonably quiet during the visit. How much is really absorbed and made part of the child's consciousness? While they are going from item to item answering the teacher's questions they may be missing the vital concept of what they are studying because their minds are flitting from one thing to another.

The Natural History Museum in London used to have a mouse beside the elephants in the main hall. As a child I was often taken there on wet days and I still am impressed by the size of the elephants compared to a mouse. I learnt then that bigness may be powerful but small is often beautiful. I can't remember much else about the museum, except to wonder at the multiplicity of living things.

This method of teaching and learning is part of Charlotte Mason's philosophy because it develops habits of attention and a reaching for perfection which remain with the children as they grow up. Every piece of work must be properly set out, handwriting must be well formed. A child who has produced two lines of good writing every day will not have an illegible hand in adulthood. No shoddy work or bad behaviour must be allowed to pass uncorrected. The teacher's expectation of her pupils' ability must be set as high as possible. Children will reach for their limit of achievement without marks. All that is necessary is encouragement and commendation.

Some may say, how can you do all this with the modern child? If the child is already spoilt it is indeed difficult but bearing in mind Charlotte Mason's maxim, 'Education is an atmosphere, a discipline and a life,' most children will eventually respond to her method of learning.

Part Two Section Four

The Science of Relations

'Education is The Science of Relations', said Charlotte Mason. A science is a logical sequence of proven facts developed from a basic idea. The Science of Relations in education follows from Charlotte Mason's first principle that a child is born a person and therefore has a right to the knowledge which will nourish his mind and develop his personality.

Each person has an innate relationship with every sphere of the sum total of knowledge available to mankind, be it knowledge of God, man or the universe. He has within himself the power to absorb much or little of this knowledge, which when presented to him in literary form becomes absorbed into his consciousness and so he becomes aware of himself as a person and a member of society.

'I am, I can, I ought, I will,' was Charlotte Mason's motto for the children. Because I am a person, so I can achieve my potential spiritually, mentally and physically. I ought to recognize the power that lies within me because I owe it to myself and to my Creator. I will make the effort to develop the relationships which are my rightful inheritance. 'You are a child of the Universe, you have a right to be here.' Christ as a boy stood among the learned men in the temple asking for knowledge. As the young person matures he is able to understand this concept of education and to realize that everyone has more within himself than is usually recognized. It is the purpose of education to draw on this latent power of mind and make it productive of knowledge. The less able has his contribution to make to society in a limited sphere, but he is not therefore to be regarded as in any way less of a personality. Charlotte Mason insisted that her philosophy and method was equally acceptable to every child, whatever his background or social status. The lilies add beauty to the field, the grass is more useful.

The achievement of a handicapped child who learns to speak or to move against tremendous odds is not less than the achievement of a gifted child who attains to the highest levels of performance. The discipline required and the personality developed in the process can be equal. Equality does not consist in the level achieved but in the effort of will and perseverance. This is the equality we should make available to the nation's young by a philosophy of education which is the science of relations and demands a discipline, an atmosphere and living ideas for its practice.

How can Charlotte Mason's philosophy be put into practice in this age when so much has changed since her day? If the basic principle of her philosophy is borne in mind it will be found that much can be done both at home and at school to carry out her principles.

Part Two Section Five

Religious Education

It is obvious from what has been said that Charlotte Mason believed in an education which did not separate the spiritual from the secular. She thought of the whole person as an entirety, the spiritual and secular complementing one another and interdependent.

All education is therefore religious education. With this thought in mind everything we do for the children is lifted out of materialism and becomes so much more worth while because it is part of the eternal plan for each individual.

We must live in the world which is real, but we could make it a fitter place for God's children through an education which draws on the powers for good.

'Goodness, truth and beauty heeding
Everyday in all we do.'

Of course the children must eventually fend for themselves in a competitive society. School is not a training ground for careers. This comes later. The most important thing about schooling is that children should know what it is to live a full, rich life, that they should face adulthood confident in the consciousness of their own potential and assured of the values that will enable them to live a good life, and with their minds full of ideas which will help them to accept what is new, yet with a regard for the past.

Every age is a new age but there is no break in the chain of history. As the children grow towards the future they are bound to the past in unbreakable links. Any new society must branch out from the roots and grow as a tree grows. Revolutionary changes are sudden outgrowths which eventually become part of the normal functioning of society. In time they become indistinguishable from the original stock.

So it is with educational theories which burst upon us as something new, which will solve all our scholastic problems. Charlotte Mason did not start something new when she reminded us that a child is a person, that education is an atmosphere, a discipline and a life, or that it is also the science of relations. All this has always been so. That man is more than flesh and blood we all know for ourselves when we are confronted with goodness, truth and beauty. Charlotte Mason was the last person to wish to be remembered as someone with a new theory. That is why her name is unknown. Her desire was to alert parents and teachers to the great truths about the mind and the personality, and to make it possible for all children to have their birthright of a full education summed up in knowledge of God, the universe and man. For Christians this must entail a study of the Bible, and for each culture a passing on to every generation of the faith which has supported and protected their particular society.

We talk glibly about a multi-racial society, a plural society, an egalitarian society (which must be the dullest of the lot) when we should be thinking beyond these terms to a society which is designed to free the individual from the restrictions of labelling and to provide for the development of the whole person, where community groupings are across the barriers which divide the young from the old, the rich from the poor, the able from the less able, the black from the white or yellow. We can see a beginning of this idea in the numerous voluntary associations which work to bring people together in caring situations, and in the communes which have sprung up in recent years. These last may seem to us to represent an extreme, but pendulums have a way of swinging. Spirituality and secularism need not be treated as separate. The things we do and the way we do them will reflect the spiritual values which are beginning to be appreciated by thinking people who see the results of the denigration of religion in a society without morals.

Part Two Section Six

In the Home

Home and school must work together, complementing and supporting one another. Parents should be encouraged to come into the schools, not only for special occasions but to meet the staff and learn about what is going on.

Teachers who live away from the area where the children live, do not know the parents, and never visit the homes, cannot be sympathetic to the problems which may arise. Caretakers and cleaners are often more aware of the environment than the teachers, and every environment has its own culture which is an important part of a child's resources for education.

A certain amount of planning and organization is necessary in the home to supplement what may be done in the school.

Young children should be read to so that they are familiar with the classics of children's literature. If the stories are talked about and the children encouraged to express their grasp of these stories in their play and in illustrations, they will make them their own. The 'let's pretend' games which have almost died out are powerful educators. Learning of verse by heart comes easily to many children as they grow out of the nursery rhyme, so a wealth of poetry can be made their own.

Parents can learn with their children and share in the pleasure of recitation. Children love to present plays and shows they themselves have prepared. Why not encourage them in a scene from one of Shakespeare's plays or their history lesson?

By all means take them out and about but prepare all visits carefully and expect some form of record to be made afterwards. Always there should be some recapitulation or report on an outing. Adults can prove to themselves how difficult it is to remember what has been seen or heard, unless some mental note is made at the time. Habits cannot be formed without regularly going over the same ground. All the things we must do are imprinted on our consciousness by continual repetition and as we learn to brush our teeth by always doing it day by day, so we can learn most things by disciplining our minds and forming mental habits. This applies equally to school work and the habit of correct presentation of work, to the habit of truthful speech and acts of kindness and consideration. There should be room for all kinds of music at home and at school so that opinions about artistic representation are based on knowledge. If a whole family can share in this way of life so much more joy will be experienced and family relationships become more closely knit.

A day in the country or by the sea will open a whole world of wonders if together young and old search for the treasures of nature. The keeping of records of the findings of these expeditions can become a lifelong hobby, and helps in the development of careful observation of details.

Charlotte Mason was not a kill-joy and would have delighted in the emancipated childhood we see around us. On the other hand she believed firmly in the self-discipline exerted in acts of consideration for others. She believed that every child had powers for good and evil, and by consistent habit training the good would flourish and the evil be controlled.

Charlotte Mason saw through class distinction and privilege to an equality that was spiritual rather than material. 'Honour all men and seek the common good,' would have been her advice to young people growing up.

Part Two — Section Seven

So to the Future

Perhaps in A.D. 2023, a hundred years after the death of Charlotte Mason, her philosophy will be acknowledged as the answer to some of our problems and children will have an education which fits them for a very short working week but enables them to occupy their leisure in such a way as to obtain satisfaction. One can visualize the development of community centres and craft workshops, the increase in theatres and concert halls, facilities for sport and the growth of interest in the preservation of the environment. All these have begun to be accepted as ways of revitalizing our inner-city areas where society is most divided and deprived.

A teacher was once asked, "What do you teach?"

Came the answer: "I try to teach the children to think."

"That," said the questioner, "is the most important thing to do."

Charlotte Mason's philosophy put into practice in the classroom will do just that and more — a delight in knowing, a search for truth and a love of beauty. What better way of fitting the children for life not only in the twenty-first century, but also the last decades of the twentieth.

It will be the responsiblity of the very gifted to make life easier for the rest of us. Therefore there must be every opportunity for the academic élite to receive the widest possible education during their formative years, or society will be faced with an inhuman machine of government controlled by robots. Science fiction has an uncanny way of becoming fact.

If we look back one hundred years and remind ourselves not only of the methods of production, transportation and communication, but also of the reasons for the growth of Trade Unionism, Socialism and the Welfare State we may be able to see a pattern of progress which changes at an ever-increasing rate. Education has become a backwater with little ripples of disturbance when someone throws in a new theory to the otherwise still waters of the *status quo*.

We need a working philosophy and Charlotte Mason would be very alive to the needs of society in the twenty-first century.